Inside My World

MY FAMILY

By Tina Benajmin

Gareth Stevens
PUBLISHING

Please visit our website, www.garethstevens.com. For a free color catalog of all our high-quality books, call toll free 1-800-542-2595 or fax 1-877-542-2596.

Library of Congress Cataloging-in-Publication Data

Benjamin, Tina.
My family / by Tina Benjamin.
p. cm. — (Inside my world)
Includes index.
ISBN 978-1-4824-1806-4 (pbk.)
ISBN 978-1-4824-1804-0 (6-pack)
ISBN 978-1-4824-1805-7 (library binding)
1. Families — Juvenile literature. I. Benjamin, Tina. II. Title.
HQ744.B45 2015
306.85—d23

First Edition

Published in 2015 by
Gareth Stevens Publishing
111 East 14th Street, Suite 349
New York, NY 10003

Editor: Ryan Nagelhout
Designer: Sarah Liddell

Photo credits: Cover, pp. 1, 5, 7, 9, 11, 13, 15, 17, 19, 21, 23, 24 (grandparents) Monkey Business Images/ Shutterstock.com; p. 24 (bike) tarasov/Shutterstock.com.

Printed in the United States of America

CPSIA compliance information: Batch #CW15GS: For further information contact Gareth Stevens, New York, New York at 1-800-542-2595.

Contents

I want you to meet my family!

I live with my mom
and dad.
These are my parents!

This is my brother.
His name is Sam.

My grandparents like
to visit.
These are
my dad's parents!

We spend lots
of time together.

Every week we eat
a big meal.
This is a family dinner.

My grandmother
cooks dinner.
My brother and I help.

Then we eat
at the table.

We go
on walks together.

My mom and dad
like to ride bikes.

Words to Know

bike

grandparents

Index